Christian Heart

Ally Doty

BookLeaf
Publishing

Presentation by *BookLeaf Publishing*

Web: www.bookleafpub.com

E-mail: info@bookleafpub.com

ISBN: 9789357446211

First edition 2023

DEDICATION

This book is for me. It's a collection of moments throughout my life that have led me to where I am now. Every moment of struggle that made even the smallest impact has changed who I am little by little. And ultimately molded me into this new person. A person I don't recognize, but someone I can't wait to know. This poetry book is for me, to cope with those struggles and to lead me into the next part of my life.

ACKNOWLEDGEMENT

Thank you to those who have supported this publication and have supported me through my twenties. This is a leap into my thirties. Even if you are not in my life anymore, you played a part. So, thank you. You know who you are.

PREFACE

Through the years of my life, I've always known myself to be a compassionate and empathetic person. We struggle as we grow and those struggles have forced me to mold myself into someone new. Come with me on a dark journey of self-discovery and growth. Who I was, is not who I am anymore.

Begin

Youth was beauty, That's what they told me. But I never felt beautiful when I was young. I was the opposite of typical, my weight was an obstacle when my adult life began.

To be young is to be alive, but what if I'm just dead on the inside? I can feel my insides begin to deteriorate and my self-awareness is naive and fragile.

Youth is confusion and delusion and degrading. You only find yourself wondering solely and waiting, for your hopes to bring you some form of delight but instead you might find a sweet damning fright.

My youth ended fast, over the last five years and adulthood is not as it seems. It gets harder the older and older you get and you somehow lose sight of your dreams.

It was people for me, who made me feel dead the longer and longer I tried, it was people who mattered the most to me that made me wish I had died.

My demons, they pick me up time and time
again but my demons have hidden affairs, they
beg me to die over and over again and whisper
sweet nothings into my ears.. .

They got meaner, as I got older, white, red and
then black, they wanted to take away all of my
pain but I struggled with them and fought back.

Caution continued, as I went on, the darker the
world would seem. I would live out my days
quite quiet and alone as if it were some
nightmarish dream.

The older I got, the harder it was to allow myself
to restart, with new people who sent me this
acknowledgment of "love"; instead I gave them
an obsidian heart.

Shame

A tear. It fell out of my eye and onto my
stomach. Onto the massive mountain that lives
under my shirt. The fear of every young woman
engulfs the shadows on my walls. My reflection
sends vulgar messages and demands a different
being to be present in it. The peach fuzz above
my navel becomes wet from the salty drops, it's
raining in my bedroom. It rained shame.

Sleeveless tops hung in my closet, never to be
seen. Never to be worn. Never to be touched by
my fragile fingers, afraid they would attract
attention to the growth protruding above my
elbows. Afraid the judgment would exude out of
the demons on the street. Afraid I would fall into
exile.

Sculpted is an antonym for the limbs that shot
down from my hips. My size twelve bottoms
barely large enough to cover the vast area of my
lower body. My skin is speckled and bunched,
looking like I sat in my oatmeal breakfast to hide
the white of my outer being. But it's just my
skin. I wear jeans to hide the deafening blows,
they silence them.

My fragile naivety broke when they laughed.
Shattered like my favorite mirror executing
every emotion that I bared. I love a man. But his
words cut me with the same shattered glass
that's on the floor. His words shrank my mind,
like Alice after drinking her wine. But the wine
only gave me more mountains I couldn't get
over.

Disgusting, overweight, unattractive; words that
poured from their lips, words that filled the
pages of my hardback journals, words that
drowned under my pen and filled my conscious
mind, words that I continued to write upon my
skin as I stared blankly at myself in the mirror. I
pull down my sleeves. I need to hide the shame.

What I see, I've grown to hate. What I crave is
unattainable. What I need, it's impossible. I
doubt myself. I will never be the blooming
flower on the porch step. I'll never have the
courage to wear sleeveless tops. Burn them, I
whisper, I'll never need them anyways.

Would the shattered pieces be enough to end it?
One fell swoop could take all the pain away, it
could ease my mind. I shake my curly dark head,
pushing the thought away. The demon in the

corner of my bedroom beckons me closer. He winks at me. I cover my head. It's not the end.

Dream

I saw two moons when I awoke, I saw two moons and no one spoke.

They hung there low inside the sky, they glowed softly like fireflies. They sat there talking about my eyes.

"They're green," one said and looked at me. "They're the deepest green of the deepest sea."

"No that can't be," the other said. I looked at him and I tilted my head. "Why, My dear," he said to me. " I see galaxies inside your eyes, can't you see it too? You must see that in yourself, you must. Your bones are made of milk and stardust."

"Galaxies?" The first moon said. "How can you be so sure? The gleam in her eyes is such a blur. I'm quite sure I see the seas, I see the seas inside of her."

They both lingered in the sky, neither of them batting an eye, for eyes seem to be the topic of choice for these two moons who had a voice.

They talked in sweet low, grumbling tones, and I felt moonlight in my bones as they drenched my hair in the night sky dreams and spoke about how my eyes gleamed.

"My friend is quite right my dear," the second Moon boomed so the world could hear. "Your eyes sparkle like the sky." He sounded hateful. I wondered why.

Solemnly he said to me, "They run deeper than your blood and soul, and somehow find the blackest holes. Your eyes see things that cannot be and they bring the worst right out of me."

"Take this star and cut them out, you don't see yourself getting out. You know that shame and hate will follow suit, cut them out from stem and root."

He bowed so deeply in the sky and thrust the star tips in my eyes. I felt myself wanting to scream but I remember this is a dream.

Blood, black like the night covers my nightshirt embedded with starlight. My vision starts to disappear and the pit of my stomach fills up with fear.

"Now you will never see yourself," his sinister tone above me fades away. "You hate yourself anyway and that is still not going to change. I leave you blind with no reason to try. The sun will be up soon, I'll let him watch you die."

I fell to my knees and they hit the water. There's no point in blinking, why even bother. My eyes are still bleeding, I sit still in the dark. Darkness, my only friend,

I woke up.

Moments

There are moments where I would deprive
myself of sunshine. I would cry, wallowing in
the white sheets of a king bed and let the grief
develop inside. It wasn't my grief, it was theirs.
Like someone I loved had just died.

There are moments when I protrude strength and
shield my heart in my hands. Guarding it from
the envious malice of grief and I would gather
their stories like sand.

There are moments when I would tear away
from the world and find myself at the edge of
the sea, demanding their grief be swept away by
every cold current that touched my feet.

It was their grief, their constant need for
validation that twisted my emotions each day. It
was always what THEY needed and wanted and
I'd give them everything I had left to say.

I had light in my eyes and people despised it, but
I simply did not even care. They never checked
in on me, but I was not a burden to bear.

I embraced the sadness they left with me and urged them to feel safe and heard. Someone once told me my feelings didn't matter and that might not be so absurd.

They came for help and love and advice that I always willingly gave, but sometimes the burden of their misfortunes tore me down deep under the waves.

I keep them in a box, all of them that once needed me or still do. Sometimes I take them out at night and read the darkest moments they went through.

And I see them now, glowing like a shiny new penny on the ground. I'm glad they're still breathing and growing and learning. Their laughter is the purest, sweet sound.

And I remember why I give parts of myself away, to give those with grief a fighting chance to stay. And I'd do it again as long as it takes to make sure they stick around. Each soul has a reason to live, as is the one that I've found.

Summer

Hello, Friend.

You remind me of summer. Your
happy-go-lucky personality took me by surprise.
We had a lot in common, you and I, the
friendship felt so innocent, I was so blind.

We shared so many moments, in and out of
work. You were young, beautiful and free, I
longed to be just like you. You were everything
to me.

You were so bold and made me believe I could
be just like you. Though I was older, you were
wiser and the sky drew warning signs in blue.

I gave you everything I was and that was my
first mistake. I wanted that same love in return, I
begged for it,our fallout was such a slow burn.
Like fire in the night lit from a soft scented
candle, I dreamt of a friendship that would grow
but it was too much for you to handle.

I made so many mistakes and confided them in
you, I thought I was teaching you to grow, but it

was you who somehow knew. That every single thing I did, was a target on my back. You shined so brightly full of love, I never had a doubt.

When I find love in friendship, it's the purest form of myself. I tend to share my hopes and dreams and give myself away. But you knew my heart was bigger than my eyes seemed to appear, you took advantage of my love as I watched you disappear.

The final blow you sent ripped my heart to shreds. I felt the knife slide further through when I was called in that day. The office was so quiet and so small when they began to speak, the lies you told them. The letter you wrote them. Unforgivable to me.

The shame and guilt I felt still lingers in my head, my skeleton is layered more so than it was before.
The first two walls to that glass box went up inside my chest, you laid the cost, but we both lost, I wish you luck with all the rest.

White

He's standing over my shoulder, looking back at me in the mirror. "See?" He said to me, "I told you, you aren't worth it."

My face is flushed, pale as can be. My fingers go numb placed on both sides of the sink. I'm sad, I'm tired, I've cried all of my tears, this is the most heart broken I have been in years.

His smile is wide like the Cheshire Cat, his demonic glare sends a shiver down my back. I know why he's here, he wants me to follow him, down to the end.. It's not time. I don't want to. I have to fight.

My shoulders droop and my eyes cast down, I turn from the mirror. With a deep, long breath I know I must go. I make no sounds and head for the door. It's time to leave.

The same demon, he follows me down to the car. His snow, white skin and his thin black heart, gets in the passenger seat next to me, he turns on the radio, it's raining.

His deep blood-shot eyes stay fixed on me. "I told you many times and I'll tell you again, no one needs you as a friend." He smirks and gleams and touches my shoulder. "There's no need to keep trying, give up, it's over."

"What if I told you it just gets worse? The people you love will fall one by one, you'll be left alone, lonely, forgotten. You don't deserve the love that you try to give, look what you've done, you're no better than them."

Maybe he's right, as I turn up the song, to drown out his words and my thoughts, but they're not gone. They swarm in my head like a hive full of bees. They sting. And sting. And sting.

New

My movements felt free, walking down the road.
It was dark for a little while, but I felt myself
grow. My friend, the demon, stays quiet but
close, his laughter inside of my head like a
ghost.

I hung my mistakes on the willows hanging over
me, like ornaments. Their tears cried for me as I
had no more to shed. They weep for my past.
And encourage my future.

My bones feel stronger, I stand taller, my heart is
bolder, my mind seems older from the lessons
I've learned over the last year, do not trust, do
not hope, but don't grow in fear.

But if I do not trust & hope, how will I grow?
How will I learn and how will I go to new
heights and find what it means to be me? I have
to have hope, won't it set me free?

I'll just keep my guard up and trust those I
know, they'll help me find happiness, they'll
help me grow. Will they? Yes, trust them.

They're family. They'll never hurt me, that
much I'm sure.

I turned my eyes to the sun and moved forward
with life. One step at a time, double, then thrice.
I didn't know what was to come, but my heart
felt so free, I found new life in myself, for once,
I was proud of me.

Spring

Hello, Friend.

You remind me of the sea; a deep, determined
soul full of mystery. It's your sweet ginger
laugh, it makes me want to laugh too. The sun
kisses your skin and leaves freckles askew.

Coffee dates and Target runs were our solace of
choice, whenever you spoke I heard the truth in
your voice. Your opinion of me sank deep in my
heart. My heart being your target, your words
were the darts.

I always felt safe when I was with you, we kept
close to each other even after I moved. But my
love and my kindness hit like your soul had a
shield, it was never enough for the friendship we
built.

We were drifting away, a slow burn over time.
I've re-written this piece with so many different
rhymes. But words can't replicate the damage
you've done, you dropped me off with an
anchor, you did it. You won.

I felt the tug grab my heartstrings over again and I knew I was losing another precious friend. Someone who held the whole world in her arms and gave me such love when I'd felt so much harm.

I gave you space and kept quiet about how I felt, I answered your calls and stayed present to help. I knew you were drowning out there on your own, a stitch in your heart like a jacket you've sewn.

But I couldn't stay quiet, not anymore. I could feel the sea pulling me closer to shore and with doubt in my heart and an explosive string, I lit a soft fuse and the truth started to sing.

I scratched at our matching tattoo on the nape of my neck and wanted it gone, it's thought made me sick. I scratched it again until it started to bleed and smothered it with sand like a treacherous weed.

And then it was time to come forth with my truth, the truth that you always seemed to abuse. Be ready, be humble, for it will take flight and this time i'll be ready to take on the fight.

Truth

And in the quiet of spring, right before summer,
I gathered my courage and I uncovered the truth.
Fuck, the truth.

It started with anger and it grew and grew like a
tornado over the water, filling itself, myself,
with more and more hatred towards you.

I typed and deleted, typed and deleted, filled up
page after page and cut and pasted. It took a
while to tone myself down, but I knew that the
whole truth would be too much and we'd drown.

Line after line, I emptied my thoughts and I
slowly felt a weight start to come off. Still
heavy, just not as heavy, like the ink in my pen,
my eyes began to darken, I was clawing at my
skin.

The itch in my heart was unbearable, I knew
once I told you, I would feel terrible. But for
whatever reason, like you, I just didn't care. I'm
so tired of fighting you. I was impaled.

I drew blood, from my heart onto the sheet, it was terrifying and immeasurably bleak. The black in my eyes shone through more and more, I wanted to fucking scream but I couldn't anymore.

It was silent. Deafeningly silent, when I reached the end. I read it over, again and again, making sure it was ready for me to send. I almost didn't, thinking I could pour the blood back into myself, but I was already exposed. It fell off the shelf.

I lunged at the screen and sent us straight to our deaths and separately we took our last final breaths. The fall was coming, the moment was still and with this deep impact, perhaps we'll never heal.

And through the foggy glass windows, you seemed to be doing so well. Hold on to those cage bars and I'll see you in hell.

Loss

In the midst of our struggle, I fell. I fell off the peak, waiting for the impact to break my bones. The wind whipped in my ears, screaming all of my faults into my mind. Replaying, over and over again like a scratched tape, the sound is nauseating.

The fall seemed never ending, but freeing. My hair engulfed my face, smothering the tears back into my eyes as I waited for the end to come. My mouth watered. Every gland reminds me of what a treacherous being I had become. Like a sore in my mouth, I was enraged. Angry. Bitter.

My hands were cold. Like ice. Catching every tilt from the wind and forcing themselves up from gravity. But I was going down.

My skin crawled. It sat there quiet and still, accepting the fate of a rash decision. Anticipating that it would stay marked on me forever.

My mind raced, after I hit send, wondering if what I had done was wrong. Was it right? I guess it didn't matter. The impact would define my choices for me.

I waited for it. For the fall to break my bones. To shatter my arms and crush my neck. For my clothes to rip and for blood to shed, but it never came. It never broke. It never ripped. It never shed.

Free

The wind silenced my thoughts. A light began to rise. The dark sky that surrounded me held me like a lover. I feel warm. I feel free. I feel a thousand stars surround me and whisper in hushed tones. "Prepare for impact." I did.

But when I hit the ground I didn't break. My bones didn't shatter. My mind didn't race. Blood didn't crawl out from under my skin and my heart didn't stop beating. I felt whole again.

It was my feet that found the floor. They touched softly in the glow of the morning dew and my knees bent ever so slightly as I found my footing again.

I looked above me. The peak was far from me. Like a mountain in the distance. Like a cloud overhead. Like the silhouette of a far off castle that could never be reached. Like an old friend.

And while the world turns, so will we. Into a deep sleep, your soul will see just what the universe made you to be.

Red

He dared me to believe in anything. His black eyes and red shell beckoning towards me. I grimace. "Like what?" I said sharply. "If I believe in something, that means I want it to be real. And if something is real, it has a greater chance of disappointing me. Why risk the idea of disappointing myself when I could have genuine absence instead?"

He smirked. The lines of his perfect red lips turning upward toward the sky. His eyes seemed to gleam at my response. His smile made me want to die.

"You believe in nothing, yet you hope for a thousand moments that will never come." He bared his teeth. He sees my grief. "Your world is burning, is this one of the thousand moments you hoped for?"

I look around. The deafening screams of burning dreams surrounded me. They were all on fire, scorching the very core of which they came from. Burning me.

But it wasn't just dreams, it was people I loved too. Yelling, screaming, begging for help, the people I once knew. But they made their choices and I cannot help them this time. I looked back at my demon, his face was grim. Ashamed. Delighted.

He looked back into my eyes and searched for my soul. It was growing much darker than it was before. I was growing empty, like the darkness in the sky, I was losing feeling, but he knew exactly why.

I was surrendering. Finally, so close to the end, just a few ties to cut, so much farther from when we began.

His eyes shone in reflection to the burning bodies and knew that I was taking my leave. I turned my back on them and listened while they screamed. They'll slowly turn to ashes and burn out like a dream.

Breaking

We tried. So hard. As husband and wife. And
that summer made me want to drift into a new
life. I was broken and hurt and so were you, we
struggled separately, but together, its true

The quiet house felt like the world stood still. A
knife cut the tension waiting to kill. There was
nothing between us for those weeks upon weeks.
There was a separation inside those walls. The
walls were breaking.

I was afraid to sleep next to you every night,
scared that I would wish all of our worries away
and pretend like nothing happened. But I
couldn't, they weren't wishing stars and the
skies were the darkest they've ever been.

I missed you. My curative mind swam through
so many emotions, so many scenarios, so many
moments of our past lives. I was swimming. I
was drowning. So were you.

I'd be fucked leaving you. I didn't want to. But I
felt I'd be fucked if I stayed.

We were so messy, like an oil painting running off in the rain. We ran around each other, leaving messes behind us. Eventually, those messes would come back and destroy us. .

And we were here. At rock bottom, the point of no return. Your sad eyes made me sadder and your broken heart broke mine more. I wanted to reach out and hold your heart in mine, but it was in a million pieces, I never saw you cry.

Is it the end? Of the world we built together? Was it time to shed my diamonds and mold into a stone? From white to gray to black, the darkness seemed a friend, now we must head towards a never-ending end.

Dreaming

Is this a dream? Where am I? Standing on a balcony overlooking the world. I see it all. New York, Beijing, Paris, London, Sydney, it's real. I can touch them.

They're unique beauty seems so distant, like viewing them on a map. But I can touch them with my fingertips, I have control.

I can smell the fresh baked croissants from Paris' desolate streets and touch the top of the monument where all the victims sleep. China's oriental beauty radiates from above, the opera house on the ocean glimpses at me. Hello. I smile.

I see you. Standing next to me, I'm so sure it's you. Isn't it? You, with your lush brown hair and your deep eyes, that mole on your chin. It's you, you're standing there holding my hand.

"I present to you, the world," he said in a calming blunder. "Everything you'll ever need, for you I surrender." My brows ruffled while I

tried to understand. "You're giving this to me?" I
let go of your hand.

"Isn't it what you want? To have everything you
dreamed? The spray of the ocean, the smell of
the trees? The wind in your face, and all the
birds that sing? You want the time that passes
and the sun and the moon, you want to write
stories in the stars, don't you?"

He was right of course, I want all of those
things. But at what cost would it seem, that I
lose everything if I dared to dream?

I gazed at the world, so full of hope and wonder
and realized it's mine if I chose to surrender. I
could climb mountains and dive into the deepest
seas, I could fly through the clouds and touch
my wildest dreams.

"All you have to do is take my hand and reach
out. We'll end those who hurt us, they're time
will run out. Don't be afraid to change the color
of your heart, come here. Lets go,"

And I woke up.

Love Letter to Me

Write a letter, she said, to each other with truth.
Write a letter with purpose and beauty and
prose. Give each other time to find the right
words but write a letter to each other, it'll help,
I'm sure.

I started mine quickly and waited to see if you
would start yours too, but you didn't and you
wouldn't and so then, I refused. So I wrote one
to myself instead, of all the things inside my
aching heart and pounding head.

Hello, me.

You remind me of darkness, a blank empty
canvas waiting for paint. You're broken and sad
and craving some life, your headstone is marked,
you've been buried alive.

Your eyes are sore and aching and wet, you just
want to sleep but the ceiling is your only
company as you try to succumb. You can't sleep.
You just toss and turn.

Images of your life are barreling through, of the life you wanted and who you once knew. You hate yourself, the moon told you so. Maybe your eyes really need to grow cold.

You never imagined your bones would break and your skin would fall off like a slithering snake. But here you are, decayed on the floor, waiting and waiting. And waiting for more.

Fear of the future melts from your heart, the black grime melts all over your shirt. It's sticky and wet and hardens like glue, start gasping for air, it'll suffocate you soon.

Don't worry darling, the ground will cave in. You'll see who you are now instead of where you've been. You'll be better for it too, just wait and see, you won't have the beating heart left to bleed.

Imagine a fog for your sight everyday, you wander and wander alone and unafraid. You're comfortable with only yourself and you disappear into your books sitting on the shelf.

Become the dark hero you love so much, stop taking the blows and start throwing the punch. Life will fuck you, that much you know. Start

taking responsibility. Oh look, it's starting to
snow.

Winter

Hello friend.

You remind me of snow. Quiet, distant, beautiful
and cold. It's your eyes of course, they're a deep
glacier blue, frozen in time like sunrises with the
moon.

Growth was imminent when I knew you, we
guided each other on trails and truth. I was
thankful to have someone I knew wouldn't
leave, I laughed at myself. What a sick joke you
believed.

Haunting laughter filled the air when we were
close, I never had to choose. I never made you
choose. Ultimatums are for cowards. I tried to
choose both of you.

The end of our time came very quick; a time
bomb, no, an atom bomb. Tick. Tick. Tick. Tick.

I can't remember what you looked like or how
you held yourself. Your heart was an icy tale,
like my favorite book on the shelf, I burned it.

I can remember your laugh though, the sound you made when you felt joy, it deafened my ears and made me feel safe. I wish I never heard it.

They're locked up memories, pushed from my mind, bottled up pieces of joy, the joy is gone and so am I. Erased. Deleted.

The snow is an emptiness that lingers, like what you meant to me. Empty doubts and unfulfilled promises, I shrug them both off. It's cold.

I smile as I write this, friendship is an empty joke. Like a sunny day before it rains. A fucking light hearted snake.

Loneliness is very much a friend to me now, comfort in chaos I've seemingly found. But the cold grows colder and my hands start to shake…Exile is near. My final mistake.

New love

I found you, my love, our house had collapsed.
You were in the rubble, you were screaming and
trapped. A small light peeked in and your hand
abruptly found mine. The mountain was steep,
but together we climbed.

We found a new love, like we hadn't before. We
grew apart, grew separately, but landed on the
same shores. We found our love was an ocean,
dangerous and deep, and I wanted to drown in
your love, so silent and so sweet.

It was sunshine and ease and profound and real,
our love rekindled, it was strong and surreal.

My heart felt alive, blood pulsed from its veins,
my demon's teeth baring, they wanted more
pain. But I couldn't find pain when I was with
you. Life was so good, so happy, brand new.

I love you, more than ever before. This felt like
a new life for both of us, I'm sure. We left all of
our mistakes buried six feet in the grave, the
same place I left my demons. I felt suddenly
brave.

I was breathing new air, I no longer choked. I could feel blood returning to my body. My heart pounded. I smiled more and more when you looked at me, you'd give me a wink, I felt finally free.

My chains fell, the world rolled off my back. Atlas and Medusa stared jealously back. The snakes slithered back into my heart, not gone, just in hiding, still ready to strike.

It took us a while, but we finally survived. Our mistakes are well behind us, our new love will thrive. No matter how black my heart comes to be, I know you'll be sitting there. Beside me.

Trying

Once again, I'm at an impasse. With those eyes
that are piercingly cold. This shit is getting so
fucking old.

I feel like I'm failing, again, so I'm told. Change
is inevitable, this I'm aware, but holding a
grudge is too much to despair.

The raven, Annabelle, a tomb by the sea, Poe
keeps me company while trying to see through
the fog and the mist that won't seem to go and
now I'm lost looking for wandering lights in the
snow.

But the lights are so dim and I can barely move,
the cold from your eyes is unbearably blue. I
thought I was doing what you wanted of me but
it doesn't matter what I do, that much I can
fucking see.

I reach out and try over and over again, but each
door is slammed in my face. You're both the
light in the snow carrying shovels and roses to
be sure that I am put in my place.

Light gray to dark gray to soot and to black, the night sky fades slowly from view. You both put in the work to silence my truth, I never thought that'd be something you'd do.

No casket, no headstone, just me in the ground, looking for any escape. Once again, giving my trust away was such a disarming mistake. Those demons of white and red lay beside me in the darkness and keep me at bay, reminding me why I simply won't matter to you at all the next day.

I shout and scream and try to be heard, but the ground keeps me silent, you kept me silent. You couldn't hear what I had to say and near the end of our time, I layed there so tired and let myself slowly decay..

Broken

They dragged me out of the frozen dark hole and
laughed as the sun hit my face, "You fucking
idiot," they mused under the trees, "You're such
a fucking disgrace," they said to me.

They giggled and rolled on the ground with glee
as I took a seat on a stump, "Must we tell you
again? You're such a shitty friend, stop giving
yourself over to them. We want you, we need
you, come play with us," I stared back and rolled
my eyes. He's starting to make sense.

I sit here cold with the snow still falling around,
I'm freezing, I'm lost and alone, but loneliness
is fondness. Oh how i've grown.

I ball up some snow in the warmth of my palm,
it shivers and melts and returns to its form. I get
to my feet, groan and roll my eyes. It hurts less
than I thought, that's a pleasant surprise.

It must be the walls that I've raised over the
years, they're tall and blockaded and made out
of steel. I trudge through the knee-high frozen

water with guilt, but why am I guilty? I ponder,
I'm still.

Perhaps it was the truth that I told, or the
moments when your eyes grew even colder, then
froze. Or when I made distance between you and
I. No wait, that was you.. I look at the sky.

What does it matter? Fuck this.

The last two walls of my heart went up with
such ease, I exhaled the warmth and my lungs
started to freeze. Death could wait a bit longer, I
know that it can. They laugh in the distance.

So I ran.

Black

It's chilly tonight, there's a knock at the door. It must be the wind, that much I'm sure. I step off the porch and look out to the sky, against the moonlight, the tree line's silhouette shines.

I see you out there, in the dark where you linger. A cloaked, lanky figure with an outstretched boney finger. Pointing my way and I know it is time, "Hello, my dear." He groans. "It's time. You're mine."

Exile, my friend, it's been way too long. Youth was beauty, they told me but my youth is long gone. Alone again, with my thoughts and my heart, Exile meets me halfway in the dark.

Paces from me, I can't see his face. His cloak is pulled up and his skin is laced with ashes and with bones carving scars like my own. He knows it is time to go on alone.

His hand reached out like a branch from a tree and I took it almost immediately. I knew he was right. It was time to go, no more time for the summer or the sea or the cold.

My memories flood the tears in my eyes.
Loneliness is no more a simple disguise.

His shadow engulfs me along with my fear, not
of him, no, of myself, it's so potently clear. Of
allowing strangers to walk into my life and
giving them pieces of me. Pieces they'll shatter
and bleed.

It's better this way, that much I'm sure. My
hollow shell walks slowly back to the door. It's
my hood now, up over my face, I'm ashes and
bone and alone in this place.

Exile is me, we're one in the same and
loneliness is now not a growing pain. Comfort is
quiet alone with a book, drinking my tea or
writing a hook. Comfort is darkness and blood
and shadows and rain and candles that burn, I
feel insanely, sane.

Exile will guide me forward from here. The
lights have gone out, it's just me in my bed. I lay
down so slowly with thoughts circling my brain,
Pennywise calls me to come down the drain.

Sleep is inevitable, I mustn't ponder anymore.
Sleep is my friend, there's another knock at the
door.

Obsidian Heart

It was midnight, in my room. Was this my room? It's too hard to tell, it's so dark. I hear something moving, in the corner over there, it slithers and groans. I'm curious, not scared.

I inch closer and suddenly I see, it's not what it's a who, it's me that I see. A different variation, here in the dark, a misinterpretation of who I should be. I look to the left, there's another of me.

I look all around, there's so many of them. From younger to older, from beginning to end. I see my past selves stand warily near, I could reach out and touch them, they're unblinkingly clear.

"What is this?" I asked, my voice shaking a bit. "We are you," the first one said. "Before you've taken your hits. Before the shit and hurt that you absorbed over time, we used to be innocent and harmless and fine. Look what you've turned us into, you fucking wretch. Now we're here in a box, in a crypt, in a ditch."

My face didn't flinch.

"The demons, they came and took pieces of you. You thought you escaped but you lost, you're through. The heart you once had is locked tightly away, now we live here, in this darkness. You'll join us one day."

My feet found the skeletons and bones on the floor, the walls covered with mirrors, there's no exit, no door. "We're dead, don't you see? We were the pieces of you that held hope and light and goodness and truth. But you've locked us away, now you're starving for hate, you hold grudges. Can't you see yourself? You're starting to shake."

I made my way over to the wall just to see myself in the mirror, while the other me's bleed, the black in this room filled my heart with delight, I creeped closer and found myself looking white.

My eyes, they were black and my fingernails too, my hair was as red as the blood that I drew. I could see my heart pumping, blood? No, it's black. It's weighing me down, it's heavy, I seem so very spent. ..

I thrust my fingers into my chest and grasp onto the one last piece of me I have left. I pull it so

44

slowly right out of my skin, it's black and heavy, it's obsidian.

I smirk and grin at myself in the dark, it's time to re-birth, it's time to re-start. I close my eyes and damn all of me to their hell, I take my black heart and bid myself a farewell.

"Let them die," I say, looking at me. "Their time is over, it's their turn to scream. Silence will accompany me from here, I have finally taken steps to embrace that fear."

I take out my blade and carve out a shape, into the heavy, dark stone that will take its place back into my chest where I won't feel a thing, the me's that surround me have started to sing.

But I cannot hear them, the steps have appeared and my demons take their places and tremble in fear. It's time to go back to the place that I know so well, my ascend is beginning. Hello, a new form of Hell.